THE FATHER'S HEART

What Heaven Has to Say About Children's Ministry

By Janice Dickey

ISBN-13: 979-8713879983

Dedication

This book is dedicated to the unsung heroes of the Body of Christ who are behind the scenes winning children to Jesus.

Special Thank You

Thank you to Whitney Yoder for helping organize my thoughts as I wrote this book. You always inspired me by helping to pull out what is in my heart and get it on paper. This book wouldn't have happened without you. Thank you to my dear friends Mary Quigley and Amy Reed for all your prayers and support, and the many hours going through the manual. I will be eternally grateful.

Table of Contents

Foreword

You have in your hands one of the best books I have ever read on children's ministry, and it's written by an amazing children's pastor. Janice was our children's pastor for over twenty years and built our children's ministry from the ground up. She has a tremendous gift from God, and the fruit produced from her efforts is evidence that she stewards it well. In our church alone, she has been instrumental in raising up so many young people who are now serving God in a variety of areas, not just at Faith Family Church but around the world. Today, she continues to be a major asset in the training, development, and growth of our current ministry, and my wife and I couldn't be more grateful.

I'm confident this book will help any church or children's pastor become better. What Janice shares on the pages that follow, we watched her live out.

Janice, from the bottom of our hearts, thank you!

Mike Cameneti
Lead Pastor
Faith Family Church, Canton OH

We've all been given authority through Christ to co-labor with Him to influence the world around us. Some have authority on a grander scale, such as business executives over large companies, and others manage individuals in a family, old and young. I teach a college class and provide therapy for children and adolescents. Every semester I have in front of me impressionable minds ready for influence. As a therapist, I talk with parents and youth that are grappling with problems that have affected their lives. My call, or choice of employment, is no different than that of a children's ministry worker. We are influencers; the words we say, behaviors we choose, gestures, and words spoken have life attached to them.

In this book, Janice tenderly lays out the elements necessary to influence a child's heart toward God. She explores the motives that guide us to care about and value even the smallest of children. She understands that children are born with a spiritual destiny; her heart and the message in this book recognizes our role as influencers toward their destiny. This book is relevant not just for children's ministry workers but for all of us that interact with young hearts and minds.

Karita Nussbaum PhD, LISW-S, LICDC

Recommendation

"I highly recommend *The Father's Heart* to anyone starting in Children's Ministry or doubting their call to Children's Ministry. Janice has years of experience ministering to children and a wealth of knowledge and wisdom that needs to be passed on to the next generation of people that will minister to children. This book truly expresses our Father's heart for reaching and discipling children. I wish I would have had this book when I was starting out over 30 years ago."

Jerry Moyer, Jubilee Gang Ministries

Why This Book?

"Let each generation tell its children of your mighty acts; let them proclaim your power." (Psalm 145:4)

Have you ever imagined what our Heavenly Father is thinking when He looks at children? I've pondered this question many times over the years because I had the amazing privilege of building a children's ministry from scratch at Faith Family Church in North Canton, Ohio. I stayed in the position of Children's Minister for 22 years. I am a graduate of Rhema Bible Training College specializing in Children's Ministry, but when I was going through the training, I always thought I would just be a helper—never the leader. I remember one of my instructors at Rhema, Judy Collins, saying, "I am training you, so you can train others." In my mind, I thought, "That is not me," and I tuned her out for the rest of the class.

Oh, how I regretted it when I found myself leading and training others how to minister to children just a few years later. I have always wondered what I missed that day! I think God has a sense of humor and I've learned over the years to never say "no" to something because you do not know what adventure God is going to take you on in your life.

Faith Family started in December 1988, and a few weeks later my mom told me that they needed someone to teach the children. The next Sunday I showed up prepared with a lesson and started teaching the grade school children. I thought it would be for a couple of weeks, but that turned

1

into 22 years of ministering to children from birth to preteen age. I would not change a thing. I like to joke that I did not hear the voice of God; I heard the voice of Mom. But the truth is, I know God called me to that place for that time.

I had no idea how to lead people in the beginning. Our pastors were very merciful to me because I made plenty of mistakes and stumbled along the way. Because of their mercy and teaching on leadership, I was able to grow as a leader as the church grew. And grow it did! It grew so fast, it was hard to keep up.

God brought some amazing people across my path to help with this precious call. I learned that **people need a vision** and a passion for what they are doing when serving in children's classes.

Over the years, I developed an orientation to first get the vision into the volunteers and help them understand the way our classes function, as well as the basics of safety and security before they start in a classroom. They needed to know how important this ministry is to Father God and why we do what we do. When they understand this, they become passionate and will stick with you in the ministry. I could name a long list of these wonderful people God brought our way who caught hold of the vision and did not let go.

As a leader, you have to keep the vision before those who serve with you. Keep reminding them of the value of what they are doing. **That is what this book is about.** There are a lot of resources on how to do children's ministry, many of which are extremely creative. **I am not addressing the "how-to" so much as the "why."**

If you were to ask any pastor, "Do you want a great children's ministry?" the answer most likely will be "yes." My challenge back would be: WHY do you want a great children's ministry? Is it because you want to attract new families to the church? (A great one will do that very thing.) Is it because you know you are supposed to have one because other churches do? Is it because you just want the children out of your hair, so they do not disturb the adult service?

I want to challenge everyone who reads this book to search the scriptures for yourself and find out what Father God has to say on the subject. What is in His heart? How important is this to Him? I hope you discover that when you reach, teach, and disciple children for the right reason, you will have an eternal impact that goes way beyond what you can see in the natural.

Unfortunately, over the years, I have witnessed children's ministry looked down upon as unimportant because it was not viewed as a real ministry. Some people would never lower themselves to work with kids because they believed their call was higher. When you come to understand that such a mindset goes against the very heart of our Father God, it will change your perspective.

Remember that this is not a career; it is a calling. This is also not a stepping stone to a better assignment. It does not mean that God will not change your assignment in the future, but you must work at this current one as if it is the most important one you will ever have.

If you are serving in or leading a children's ministry, please do not be critical of your pastor or church leadership if you believe they do not fully grasp the importance of ministering to children. It is not your job to correct leadership, but you can pray for them and remain faithful.

My prayer as you read this book is that you will gain insight into what really is in our heavenly Father's heart when it comes to ministering to children. As you will see in the following pages, we have such a limited amount of time to really impact their lives. May we not waste these precious God-ordained opportunities to make a difference in the life of a child.

"Red and yellow, black and white, they are precious in His sight. Jesus loves the little children of the world."[1]

Discussion Question

1. If you grew up attending a church, reflect on your experience being taught and ministered to as a child. What impact did it have on you?

Chapter 1
The Challenge We Face

"...Go to all people everywhere in the world. Tell God's good news to everyone." (Mark 16:15 EASY)

A good friend of mine, Pastor Tom Toney, shared this illustration: If you were given a lump of playdough and asked to make the shape of a person, it would be easy to do because it is soft and pliable. However, if you were given a rock and asked to form the same shape, it would be much harder to do—maybe even impossible. This is how it is with a child.[1] The time to mold and shape children to follow God's plan for their life is when they are easy to teach and pliable. When is that? As you will soon discover, it is before the age of 13.

There is a great battle for the hearts of our children happening right now. The children of today are facing an unprecedented onslaught from the enemy of lies and deception at a very early age, even as young as preschool. What is being promoted as cultural acceptance and diversity goes against all of the principles of God that we see in His Word. Truth be told, what is currently acceptable in our culture is just plain old sin masquerading as love and acceptance.

Other cultures and religions know they have to establish their beliefs in children from the very earliest years in order to have a committed believer for their entire lives. Yet, very often in Christianity, we have missed it. We have failed to understand how vital it is to establish belief in God and faith in God as soon as possible. The thinking has been that children are too young to understand or that they must wait until they are older to have a relationship with God. **What are your thoughts on this subject? Have you ever considered a person's age to be a factor in them having a relationship with God?**

A person's worldview is largely formed during the crucial elementary years of ages 5 to 12. What is a worldview? It is the lens by which you perceive the world and unconsciously make decisions. If we want a child to have a scripturally-based worldview, we cannot wait until they are older because influence is happening whether we realize it or not. If we are not influencing them with the truth of God's Word, the world will be influencing them with wrong thinking patterns. This influence can come through TV, music, video games, school teachers and curricula, friends, social media, and ungodly lifestyles.

The National Association of Evangelicals found that a whopping 63% of the Christian adults they polled were saved during the "4/14 window," between the ages of 4 and 14.[2] Here are some other startling statistics from George Barna's book *Transforming Children into Spiritual Champions*:

- "We discovered that the probability of someone embracing Jesus as his or her Savior was 32 percent for those between the ages of 5 and 12; 4 percent for those in the 13- to 18-age range; and 6 percent for people 19 and older. In other words, if people do not embrace Jesus Christ as their Savior before they reach their teenage years, the chance of their doing so at all is slim."

- Regarding ages 5 to 12: "Why focus on this particular slice of the youth market? It is during these crucial eight years that lifelong habits, values, beliefs, and attitudes are formed."

- "By the age of 13, your spiritual identity is largely set in place."[3]

You can see from these studies that the **most effective** field of evangelism is winning children to Jesus. If you want to look at it from a monetary standpoint, it is a better return on your investment. It is so much easier to get someone saved before the age of 12 than at any other time in their life.

According to The World Bank's statistics for 2019, children ages 0 to 14 make up about a quarter of the world's population.[4] If we really care about winning the lost and expanding the kingdom of God, we will place a high priority on reaching, teaching, and discipling children to become lifelong followers of Christ.

We are living in the last days as foretold in Scripture. We have a limited time to guide children into a relationship with their heavenly Father and teach them to be disciples of our Lord Jesus. Not only are we limited in the time remaining before Jesus returns, but the window of opportunity to form a child's worldview based on Scripture is also limited. Now is the time to wake up to the challenge we face when it comes to today's children and our responsibility to do something about it.

Today's generation lives in a culture driven by social media and technology like never before in history. It affects every aspect of their lives. Their sense of self-worth and connection to others is dependent upon this culture. Unfortunately, we often hear of a preteen or even a child who took their own life because of online bullying. Their lives are snuffed out before they hardly began. It is an irrevocable consequence of a short-term problem that they cannot see past. How can we help children combat this culture and see themselves as our heavenly Father sees them? How can we help them understand the good things He has available for them?

> **Jeremiah 29:11** "'...For I know the plans I have for you,' says the Lord. 'They are plans for good and not for disaster, to give you future and a hope.'"

The battle is on! We cannot run from it. Time is of the essence! The enemy is after our children. One of his strategies has been to lull Christians into thinking that there is plenty of time to influence our children. We must not let the devil win when it comes to the children we have an opportunity to influence.

Our ministry team understood that we could not settle for just 32 percent of the children accepting Jesus as their Lord and Savior—we aimed for 100 percent. **We did not want one child to move on to the youth group**

without being saved. To work towards this goal, we presented the gospel to the children in each class, giving them frequent opportunities to respond when they were ready to make a genuine heartfelt decision.

> **John 4:35b (TPT)** "Look at all the people coming—now is harvest time! For their hearts are like vast fields of ripened grain—ready for a spiritual harvest."

Courtney's Story

"I remember being about four years old in Bible class and listening to my teacher talk about Jesus. She spoke of how He died on the cross for everything I did wrong, and because He did that, all I needed to do was invite Him into my heart to be forgiven. And the best part was I would get to spend all eternity in heaven with Him and my family. I accepted the invitation and invited Jesus into my heart right then and there. I felt my heart fill up with such love and peace, knowing that I belonged to Him! A few years later, I was at a meeting in church. We had a guest minister, and I was sitting in the big service where all the adults were. I was having trouble with my neck hurting all the time, and this minister said that Jesus wanted to heal my body! I went up to the front of the sanctuary, and he prayed for me and a bunch of other people, too. When he prayed and touched my head,

I felt the healing anointing flow through me—all the way to my toes! It was warm, and it was SURGING through me! I almost couldn't keep still! When I went home, I realized I was completely healed. I never had that pain again. That's when I really realized just how much Jesus loved me. He not only saved me, He healed me! I am so thankful for the day I invited Him into my heart." — *Courtney Jacobs, Worship Leader*

Discussion Questions

1. As a church, are your evangelism efforts directed at the 4/14 window that is discussed in this chapter?

2. Are most of the children who attend your Children's Ministry given the opportunity to receive salvation before they move on to your youth group?

Chapter 2
Our Heavenly Father's Perspective
"...Let the children come to me..." (Mark 10:14b)

Have you ever searched the Bible to find out what Father God's thoughts are on what ministering to children should look like? If we want to know His perspective, then we need to take a look at Jesus' ministry here on earth.

Jesus repeatedly said, "If you've seen me, you've seen the Father." In other words, Jesus' actions and words are showing us exactly what is in the heart of our Father God. Take a look at some instances where He said this:

> **John 14:9b, 11** "...Anyone who has seen me has seen the Father... Just believe that I am in the Father and the Father is in me. Or at least believe because of the work you have seen me do."
>
> **John 5:19** "So Jesus explained, 'I tell you the truth, the Son can do nothing by himself. He does only what he sees the Father doing. Whatever the Father does, the Son also does.'"
>
> **Luke 9:46-48** "Then the disciples began arguing about which of them was the greatest. But Jesus knew their thoughts, so he brought a little child to his side. Then he said to them, 'Anyone who welcomes a little child like this on my behalf welcomes me, and anyone who welcomes me also welcomes my Father who sent me. Whoever is the least among you is the greatest.'"

Matthew 18:1-5 "About that time the disciples came to Jesus and asked, 'Who is greatest in the Kingdom of Heaven?' Jesus called a little child to him and put the child among them. Then he said, 'I tell you the truth, unless you turn from your sins and become like little children, you will never get into the Kingdom of Heaven. So anyone who becomes as humble as this little child is the greatest in the Kingdom of Heaven. 'And anyone who welcomes a little child like this on my behalf is welcoming me.'"

Their argument was over who would be the greater one when Jesus sets up His kingdom. To answer this question, Jesus brought a young child over to show the Father's perspective on who is the greatest. This was a radical shift in their cultural mindset. Children were the lowest of importance in their society, but Jesus elevated them by revealing the Father's heart. Let's take a look at another incident that demonstrates this point.

Mark 10:13-16 (*emphasis mine*) "One day some parents brought their children to Jesus so he could touch and bless them. But the disciples scolded the parents for bothering him. When Jesus saw what was happening, he was ***angry*** with his disciples. He said to them, 'Let the children come to me. Don't stop them! For the Kingdom of God belongs to those who are like these children. I tell you the truth, anyone who doesn't receive the Kingdom of God like a child will never enter it.' Then he took the children in his arms and placed his hands on their heads and blessed them."

This is one of my favorite portions of Scripture. Try to imagine what was happening here. Everywhere Jesus went, thousands of people would come to hear Him, to be healed or to touch Him or get something from Him. Jesus trained the disciples to help organize the people. They kind of acted like our church ushers. Picture this: here is Jesus, doing the important "Jesus work" of teaching, preaching, and healing. But right in the middle of it, here come the mommies and the daddies, and grandmas and the grandpas bringing their little children to Jesus. All they wanted was a blessing for their children and for them to meet this amazing man. The disciples viewed this as a major interruption to the "real" ministry, so they stopped the parents and scolded them. Jesus saw what was happening and stopped what He was doing to correct the disciples. In fact, Jesus rebuked them. This is a really strong term. Jesus was **angry** with the disciples for stopping the children from coming to Him. He did not say in a sweet voice, "Now, now, My disciples, we shouldn't do that." He spoke strongly and sternly with them. Remember the scripture said He was **angry**.

He then took time with each and every child to hold them in His arms, talk to them, and bless them. Don't you just love this about our Savior? He placed such a high value on children and demonstrated by His actions that the Father desires for even the littlest of children to have a relationship with Him.

Here are some recorded instances in the gospels when we see Jesus upset or angry:

- When He cleaned out the temple (Matthew 21:12-13)
- When He rebuked the scribes and Pharisees (Matthew 23)
- When the disciples turned away the children (Mark 10:13-16)

In the temple incident, what the vendors were doing was disrespectful and dishonoring to Father God and His house. Their purpose was to make a profit off of the people who were sincerely trying to do what they were commanded to do, which were annual trips to the temple to offer a sacrifice. It must have looked like a circus in the temple. Can you imagine what the children heard and saw when they walked into that scene? What impression that would have left on them?

When Jesus spoke so strongly to the scribes and Pharisees, it is because they were just about religion and not relationship. Their tedious rules were a burden and a hardship to the people who could never fulfill these many laws. How could the people ever expect God to receive their sacrifice or be confident that they could approach Him?

What do these three incidents have in common? They each show Jesus correcting the actions of people who were hindering others from coming to Father God and having a relationship with Him.

Now let's look at when Jesus warned against causing a child to stumble.

> **Matthew 18:6** "But if you cause one of these little ones who trusts in me to fall into sin, it would be better for you to have a large millstone tied around your neck and be drowned in the depths of the sea."
>
> **Mark 9:42** "But if you cause one of these little ones who trusts in me to fall into sin, it would be better for you to be thrown into the sea with a large millstone hung around your neck."

Wow! Jesus basically said you are better off dead than messing with one of His children by causing them to stumble or fall into sin. I did not say this—Jesus did. Think about it. It is a very sobering thought.

How do we cause a child to stumble? One of the first ways is by how we live. Children are watching all the time. As those who minister to children, we set an example. If we are hypocrites, saying one thing and doing another, they see it. If we praise the Lord and act holy in church but live contrary to the Word during the week, they may see it. We are always teaching them whether we know it or not. Why would a child want to accept Jesus as their Savior and live for Him if the example set before them is inconsistent? As Charles Spurgeon said, "Train up a child in the way he should go—but be sure you go that way yourself."[1]

We can also cause children to stumble or sin by not carefully guarding what is allowed into their hearts. Our eyes and ears are how things are planted into our hearts. Sometimes a cartoon, TV show, movie, or video game seems innocuous to us, but they are often very deceptive and are being used as tools by the enemy to lead children into sin and an ungodly worldview. That can be a stumbling block and has no place in church.

I believe we can also cause children to stumble and even turn away from the things of God by praying pacifying, faithless, unscriptural prayers. One time, one of the associate pastors at our church went to pray for a little girl who was in the hospital with many health challenges. He asked if he could pray for her. She turned away from him because she didn't want prayer. Why? I believe it is because too many faithless prayers had been prayed over her by others with no results to those prayers. As a result, she did not believe in prayer and wanted nothing to do with it.

However, children who have experienced faith-filled prayers that bring results from heaven are eager to pray. My niece, Whitney, was three years old when I had the brilliant idea to take her along with another niece and nephew to an indoor play zone with slides and ball pits for a day of fun.

One of the children needed to go to the bathroom, so I took them all in together since they were little. When one child closed the stall door, I did not realize that little Whitney had her hand in the doorway by the hinge. The door was accidentally slammed shut on Whitney's knuckles. She immediately began to scream! It took a little bit, but I was finally able to get the other child to open the door from the inside. Whitney was then able to pull her hand out, but it was flattened across the knuckles and very red. She screamed and cried! I got an ice pack, but it didn't help. I could not get her calmed down until I said, "Let's pray!" She immediately quit crying and stuck her little hand out for me to pray. I prayed, and she went right back to playing. The knuckles plumped back up, and there was no red mark or bruising. God answered this prayer and healed her hand. I have to admit, I really believe it was Whitney's faith that received the healing and not mine. I was worried about what her parents would say because Auntie Jannie let their baby girl get hurt. Whitney had already experienced faith-filled prayers. At only three years of age, she knew that asking Father God for help worked.

Look at what this verse says in **Matthew 18:14**: "In the same way, it is not my heavenly Father's will that even one of these little ones should perish." This speaks so beautifully of our Father's heart, and it absolutely melts me. It expresses His desire for the children to really know Him and spend eternity with Him.

Mark 16:15 says, "And then he told them, 'Go into all the world and preach the Good News to everyone.'" This is a command, not an optional request. While we are going about obeying this directive given by our Lord Jesus, we need to include reaching children because in following the Father's heart, Jesus intentionally included them in His ministry.

Whitney's Story

"I received Christ when I was around four or five years old. I had been hearing about receiving Jesus at church and from my mom. She let me know that she could pray with me whenever I was ready to receive Him. One day, while I was playing with some toys at my house, I sensed God tugging on my heart to receive Him. I thought, "I'll do that later," but I kept sensing His tugging, so I went to my mom while she was doing laundry and I told her that I wanted to ask Jesus into my heart. We knelt down on the living room floor, and she led me in a prayer of salvation.

Years later, when I was around ten years old, I attended a church meeting where Brother Kenneth E. Hagin was speaking. At the altar call, I had a very strong sense in my heart that I should respond. I started bawling because I felt so touched by God. My head didn't understand why God was asking me to go forward since I knew I was already saved, but my heart knew it was God asking me to respond.

I have so many positive memories from attending Children's Church. We had fun as we learned about God. There were so many fun games and competitions. We sang songs; we danced; we watched puppet shows. I also remember times of worship in Children's Church when the Holy Spirit's presence was so strong.

I don't remember having my hand crushed while we were at the indoor play zone, but I believe I had a simple, childlike faith because of what I had been taught. My family always prayed for healing when we got hurt or sick. Children can easily experience the things of God because they simply believe what they are told. They don't let their reasoning get in the way. What a valuable treasure to learn about the things of God from a young age." — *Whitney Yoder*

Discussion Questions

1. Are we providing a welcoming atmosphere for families that reflects how Father God feels about Children's Ministry?

2. Are our children receiving the same type of faith-filled teachings as the adults in our church?

3. Could our actions outside of church and on social media be a stumbling block to children?

Chapter 3
The Responsibility of the Church and the Family

"We will not hide these truths from our children; we will tell the next generation about the glorious deeds of the Lord..." (Psalm 78:4)

Former President Ronald Reagan once stated, "Freedom is never more than one generation away from extinction. We didn't pass it to our children in the bloodstream. It must be fought for, protected, and handed on for them to do the same."[1]

What is true for our constitutional freedoms is also true for our Christian beliefs. Just like the freedoms we have will not be preserved without intentionality, our children will not learn to live as Christians if we do not intentionally train them up in faith. We cannot be passive and expect them to live for Christ if they have not been taught who He is and what He has done.

I have heard parents say that they are going to let their children choose what they want to believe when they get older. Understandably, we are not to force children to believe in Jesus, but we must teach them the way to Christ and how to have a relationship with Him. If we do not, we are leaving a void in their lives. In the absence of Truth, the kingdom of darkness and the way of the world will influence our children. **If we leave a God-void in our children's lives, the devil will fill it.**

In the following passage, found in the Gospel of John, we see Jesus giving instructions to Peter. We could look at this passage and only see it as Jesus giving Peter three chances to redeem himself since he denied Jesus three times. I think there is a whole lot more going on here. This is the Chief Pastor (Shepherd) Jesus, giving instructions to Pastor Peter, one of the first pastors in the new Body of Christ.

> ### John 21:15-17 *(emphasis mine)*
> "After breakfast Jesus asked Simon Peter, 'Simon son of John, do you love me more than these?'
> 'Yes, Lord,' Peter replied, 'you know I love you.'
> **'Then feed my lambs,'** Jesus told him.
> Jesus repeated the question: 'Simon son of John, do you love me?'
> 'Yes, Lord,' Peter said, 'you know I love you.'
> '**Then take care of my sheep**,' Jesus said.
> A third time he asked him, 'Simon son of John, do you love me?'
> Peter was hurt that Jesus asked the question a third time. He said, 'Lord, you know everything. You know that I love you.'
> Jesus said, '**Then feed my sheep**.'"

This event occurred right before Jesus returned to heaven. If you are an employer or a parent who is going away for a while, you leave instructions for things that need to be done in your absence. Most of the time, the most important instructions are reiterated again right before you leave. That is what Jesus was doing here. Notice that Jesus gave Peter three distinct instructions.

The first thing Jesus said was, "Feed my lambs." The lambs are the little ones. This includes new believers who are spiritual babies, but "lambs" literally refers to little or young sheep. The little ones are children. When Jesus says, "Feed my lambs," He is telling us that we need to feed children spiritually with the Word of God. If Jesus said it was important for His lambs to be fed, then we must take seriously our responsibility to teach and train children in the way they should go. This is the Father's heart.

Let's see what else the Word has to say about this subject.

Psalm 78:4-8 "We will not hide these truths from our children; we will tell the next generation about the glorious deeds of the Lord, about his power and his mighty wonders. For he issued laws to Jacob; he gave his instructions to Israel. He commanded our ancestors to teach them to their children, so the next generation might know them—even the children not yet born—and they in turn will teach their own children. So each generation should set its hope anew on God, not forgetting his glorious miracles and obeying his commands. Then they will not be like their ancestors—stubborn, rebellious, and unfaithful, refusing to give their hearts to God."

When the people of Israel forgot what God did for them and did not obey His commands, they became stubborn, rebellious, and unfaithful, and they refused to give their hearts to God. They stopped passing the truth on to the children, and they got into trouble. The same applies to our children; a lack of teaching of God's truth, and a failure to allow them to experience His glory and power through worship, prayer, and fellowship with Him produces children and teens who are stubborn and rebellious toward God and disconnected from the faith.

This is not just the responsibility of the church. It is also the responsibility of the family. **This is where pastors come in** by teaching parents how to lead their own families.

Oftentimes, parents look to the church to teach their children about God and the faith. The truth is that the spiritual welfare of their children is primarily their responsibility. However, many of them do not understand this, or they are intimidated by it, especially if they are new believers, so they expect the church to take care of this for their child.

Now there is a disturbing trend in many modern churches today. They believe that since it is the responsibility of the parent to teach and train their children that the church does not need to make that their focus. They have turned their children's classes into nothing more than fun and entertainment. There is no solid teaching of the Word or exposure to the corporate anointing.

Some of the children coming to our classes are burdened and broken because of their home and family situations. Only the Holy Spirit knows exactly what they need and how to minister to them, so **make room for the Holy Spirit in your classes**. Give space for Him to work in their hearts. Let's be intentional not to rush these moments. What can these moments look like? Maybe it is quiet time after worship, allowing children to come forward and kneel at the altar or kneel at their chairs to talk to God. Maybe it is allowing time for their teachers and leaders to pray with them one on one. If you are the leader of that class, you have to get direction from the Heavenly Father for yourself on what it should look like because each church and local culture are different.

The compounded effect of children learning about God through witnessing their parents' walk of faith and learning lessons targeted for their age group along with the corporate anointing at church is powerful! **It takes the Church and the family working together** to impact and mold the lives of children, so they will choose a relationship with Christ and serve Him for all of their lives.

Teaching families the truths from scriptures like these from Deuteronomy will help equip them to lead their own children spiritually.

> **Deuteronomy 6:5-7 (*emphasis mine*)** "And you must love the Lord your God with all your heart, all your soul, and all your strength. And you must commit yourselves wholeheartedly to these commands that I am giving you today. **Repeat them again and again to your children. Talk about them when you are at home and when you are on the road, when you are going to bed and when you are getting up**."

Deuteronomy 6:6-7 (MSG, *emphasis mine*)
"Write these commandments that I've given you today on your hearts. **Get them inside of you and then get them inside your children**. Talk about them wherever you are, sitting at home or walking in the street; talk about them from the time you get up in the morning to when you fall into bed at night."

Deuteronomy 4:9-10 "But watch out! Be careful never to forget what you yourself have seen. Do not let these memories escape from your mind as long as you live! And be sure to pass them on to your children and grandchildren. Never forget the day when you stood before the Lord your God at Mount Sinai, where he told me, 'Summon the people before me, and I will personally instruct them. Then they will learn to fear me as long as they live, and they will teach their children to fear me also.'"

We are clearly instructed to make the Word of God an integral part of our lives, not only for our benefit but for the benefit of our children. **When our faith is woven into the fabric of our lives, our children will see and hear us live out what we believe**. That is why the Scripture says to talk about God's Word all the time. First, we get the Word in us, then we get it into the children. It is an ebb and flow in our daily lives to commune with God, commune with our kids, and show them how to commune with God for themselves.

Proverbs 22:6 (NKJV) "Train up a child in the way he should go, and when he is old he will not depart from it."

I know from my personal experience how much I learned by observing my parents live out their faith. For example, I learned to tithe and be generous by watching my parents. They consistently gave money to the church, missionaries, and other evangelical works. They never missed an opportunity to give. It was just who they were, and I saw God bless them in return because He could trust them with finances. They believed that they were to be a conduit to funnel finances into advancing the kingdom of God. So being a generous person who tithes and gives money to various ministries was easy for me because I learned from my family that being generous was a part of who we are.

Going to church every week without fail was something I learned from my family as well. My dad always said that going to church was what refreshed and recharged him for the rest of the week, especially during the early years of launching his business. Being fed spiritually is what sustained him through all of the ups and downs. So, from my dad, I learned the value of being fed spiritually under a pastor. I count it a blessing that I was trained up in these ways.

I also remember hearing my dad sing and praise the Lord at home. It was a part of who he was. There was something so comforting to me to hear him walking down the hallway singing to the Lord. He could not sing a lick, but that didn't matter. It does not matter to the Lord how you sound. He is just looking for the heart that is truly worshipping Him. My dad's example of worshipping God affected me.

My mom taught me how to speak Scripture over myself when it came to school and studying for exams. I still have the little notecard where she wrote those scriptures out for me. This invaluable truth has stayed with me my whole life.

Where did my parents learn these things? They learned it from their pastor through the Word that he taught and through their own fellowship with Father God.

When we live out what we believe, allowing our children to witness us praying and getting answers to prayer, when they hear us praising and worshipping the Lord, when they see us look to Scripture for guidance and answers to problems we face, it makes our faith relational. They can identify with it. At the same time, it teaches them how to get their own answers from God's Word and by prayer.

Reverend Ken Blount shared, "As a parent, the greatest teacher your children have is the life for Christ you are living in front of them, through the good and bad times in life."[2]

We cannot neglect the spiritual welfare of our children. The responsibility is on all of us to carry out what is so precious to our Father. If we do not want to see Christianity pass away with the next generation, we must follow Jesus' instructions and feed His lambs and teach them how to have their own relationship with Him.

As Pastor Kenneth W. Hagin said, "Each generation has got to have their own experience with God. Your kids and grandkids cannot survive on your generation's experience."[3]

Josh's Story

"I will never forget the day I accepted Jesus. I was four years old, and my parents were talking to me about Jesus and about asking him to come into my heart and be my Lord and Savior. I had heard about Jesus many times at home from my parents and the Christian shows they'd play for me and the Bible on cassette they'd play every night when I went to bed. I also heard stories about Jesus in Children's Church. I remember telling my mom that I wanted to receive Jesus. She and my dad led me in the prayer right then and there.

I'm so thankful for parents that raised me in the things of God and a church that ministers to kids on their level. My church and our children's pastor always treated it as a MINISTRY, not just "watching the kids while the adults are in church." We had church. The combination of godly parents and growing up in a church that prioritizes children's ministry is what helped me become the passionate follower of Jesus that I am today.

I was filled with the Holy Spirit at the age of nine. I was in Children's Church, and the teacher was talking about there being more—that you could be filled with the Holy Spirit and the evidence would be speaking in other tongues. He said there's more of the Holy Spirit you can have. Something stirred in me. I knew that if there was more, I wanted more! That Sunday morning in 1992, I was filled with the Spirit and have been speaking in tongues ever since. I'm now in my 30s, and praying in the Spirit has become such an essential part of my daily life!" — *Josh Pancher, Campus Pastor*

Discussion Questions

1. As a ministry, what has been our attitude about children's ability to receive and walk in the truths of God's Word?

2. Do the children we minister to exhibit that their faith is developing because of our example and teaching?

3. Can you think of someone who has poured into your life in some way? How did that affect you or change your life?

Chapter 4
How Young is Too Young?

"When I heard your greeting, the baby in my womb jumped for joy."
(Luke 1:44)

Over the years, there has been some debate in churches about what is an appropriate age for sharing the Gospel with children. It is easy to only look at a child's physical and emotional development. Sometimes, we are so caught up in the everyday tasks of teaching them to tie their shoes or learn their a-b-c's that it is all we can see. **However, children are first and foremost spirit beings,** so we also need to look at their spiritual capabilities and development. A good start to this discussion would be to ask yourself at what age do you think children can begin responding to God, or when can they begin to grasp the truths from God's Word? I suggest to you that the best way to answer these questions is to look in the scriptures.

Luke 1:39-44 "A few days later Mary hurried to the hill country of Judea, to the town where Zechariah lived. She entered the house and greeted Elizabeth. At the sound of Mary's greeting, Elizabeth's child leaped within her, and Elizabeth was filled with the Holy Spirit. Elizabeth gave a glad cry and exclaimed to Mary, 'God has blessed you above all women, and your child is blessed. Why am I so honored, that the mother of my Lord should visit me? When I heard your greeting, the baby in my womb jumped for joy.'"

Isn't it interesting that a baby who was still in his mother's womb was the first one to recognize Jesus? This baby responded to His presence. In fact, he "jumped for joy." Allow me to share my own story.

One night, during the time my mother was pregnant with me, my parents were lying in bed, talking to God and seeking answers about the Holy Spirit. All of a sudden, they both sensed the warmth of God's presence flowing from the top of their heads down through their bodies to their feet. My mom said when the warmth reached her belly that I began to jump and kick in her womb. Again, **even babies respond to the presence of God**.

Here is a sweet story that happened with my great-niece. Every time she comes to my house, she asks me to tell her about Jesus and how He died on the cross and rose from the dead. I also share with her how Jesus is coming back someday to take us to heaven. One day, when she was just four years old, as I was talking about Jesus, she said with tears in her eyes, "I miss Him," then she got a surprised look on her face because she wasn't expecting to say that. It hit me so profoundly because I realized that statement came out of her spirit. Her little spirit came from the Father of Spirits, and her spirit is still alive unto God, so of course she misses Him!

In the book of 1 Samuel, we read the account of how Hannah dedicated her child to the Lord, and he began to serve in the temple from a very young age.

> **1 Samuel 2:18** "But Samuel, though he was only a boy, served the Lord. He wore a linen garment like that of a priest."

I love that God did not disqualify Samuel from serving in the House of the Lord just because he was so young. Samuel was being trained by Eli, a prophet and a priest. However, Eli was unable to correct his own sons. They dishonored the sacrifices people brought to the Lord and committed horrible sins. Because of this, God was not able to speak through Eli like He should have been able to, so God went to a boy.

Verse 26 says, "Meanwhile, the boy Samuel grew taller and grew in favor with the Lord and with the people."

The Lord sent another man of God to speak correction to Eli about his sons. What they were doing was so serious and evil that God said they would die and, "Then I will raise up a faithful priest who will serve me and do what I desire. I will establish his family, and they will be priests to my anointed kings forever" (**1 Samuel 2:35**).

The faithful priest God had in mind was the boy, Samuel. Think about it. At that time, there were no other adults in the temple who were listening to God. Even at an early age, Samuel demonstrated a love and respect for God and His temple. God began to use Samuel from that point on.

In 1 Samuel 3, we read how the Lord called out to Samuel one night. The boy didn't recognize the voice of the Lord yet. He went to Eli and asked him what he wanted, but Eli said he didn't call him and told him to go back to bed. This happened three times. Finally, Eli gets a clue that it is the Lord that is talking to Samuel, so he instructs Samuel on how to respond to the Lord.

Samuel was ready and willing as a young child to be used by God. Once he knew the voice of God and responded to it, God was able to use him to speak His Word to the people. This was the start of his journey as the prophet of God. Think about the weight of what God entrusted young Samuel with that night and the responsibility that went with it. **Did Father God consider Samuel to be too young?**

Let's take a look in the New Testament at what Paul has to say. In Romans 7:9 (NKJV), Paul says, "I was alive once without the law, but when the commandment came, sin revived and I died."

The *New Living Translation* says, "At one time I lived without understanding the law. But when I learned the command not to covet, for instance, the power of sin came into my life and I died."

The Apostle Paul is teaching us that the spirits of children start out alive to God from the womb, but at some point in their lives, they come to the knowledge of sin. That is when their spirit dies or "sin revives." We call this the age of accountability.

I personally believe this occurs at a different age for each child depending on what they have been taught and the opportunities to which they have been exposed. Charles Spurgeon once said, "A child of five, if properly instructed, can, as truly believe, and be regenerated, as an adult."[1] In my experience, some children as young as four can actually understand their need for a Savior. I have witnessed their genuine conversions. These early experiences should not be discounted. We, as adults, are responsible for the truth we hear, and so are children. **There is mercy on them when they are young, but at some point, they have to choose Jesus.**

During my years as a Children's Pastor, I have come to realize there are several reasons why children may respond multiple times to an invitation. They are hearing the voice of the Holy Spirit, and that is why they feel drawn to come forward when there is something in their life that needs prayer. For instance, they may be under conviction for a sin they committed, and they need to ask for forgiveness. They may be going through something with a family member and want prayer for that situation. They may need healing in their body and want prayer. It is our responsibility to listen to them and find out why they responded, and pray with them accordingly. This will help us discern who came for the first time to receive Jesus as their Lord and Savior.

When I was six years old, my parents took us to a tent meeting held by a traveling evangelist, Ralph Morton. The tent was out in a farm field. I remember being tired of sitting, and after a while, I got down in the grass to play. As long as I was quiet, my parents let me be. I don't remember the songs that were sung or the message that was preached, but when the minister began to give the altar call, I stood up. I knew I was supposed to go down front. I told my dad I wanted to go down there. He moved his legs aside and let me through. I remember kneeling with the adults down at the altar bench. It was not until I was an adult that I found out that my sister, who is 18 months older than me, responded the same night.

When I went back to my seat, I knew something was different. I remember what the sky looked like. I remember the dress I was wearing (pink with a white collar and a silk rose in the center). When the service was over, while the grown-ups were talking, I stood outside and just looked at the sky. Something had changed in me, and I knew it. I could not give you the theological, scriptural explanation of what had happened to me, but I knew that what I had experienced was real. I don't remember a whole lot else of what happened in my life at that age, but I remember that night. I was not a horrible sinner at age six, but Romans 3:23 says, "For everyone has sinned; we all fall short of God's glorious standard." The sin nature is in us all until we accept Jesus as our Lord and Savior.

What if my parents had said, "Janice, you weren't even paying attention," or, "You're too young and don't know what's going on"? It would have prevented me from responding to God that night. **How many times in Christian circles have we kept children from responding to God because we thought they were too young or that they did not understand what they were doing?**

In **Matthew 18:10** Jesus states, "Beware that you don't look down on any of these little ones. For I tell you that in heaven their angels are always in the presence of my heavenly Father." This scripture challenges us to examine our hearts and our motives when it comes to ministering to children and our understanding of their spiritual capacity. If we disregard a child's experience with the Lord, or we believe they are unable to receive things of a spiritual nature, we are looking down on them. "Looking down" does not refer to being taller than a child. It is referring to a position of haughtiness or superiority. As we can see, Jesus did not "look down" on children.

About three years after the tent meeting, we had a revival meeting at church. I really liked the minister as I had heard him before. My sister and I enjoyed their family music records and played them on our little record player every night. (Yes, I am "record player" old.) The first night, the evangelist gave the altar call, and I sensed such a strong conviction that I was supposed to respond. I was so confused because I was sure I was saved. I did not understand why I was feeling this way. I hesitated because it mattered to me if my friends thought I was not already saved. I let peer pressure keep me from responding.

That night, when we went home, I was under such conviction by the Holy Spirit that I could not even stand to listen to the music album like usual. I was miserable. The next night we were back in church, and I was dreading the altar call. Sure enough, the conviction got even stronger on me until I finally raised my hand. I went forward and knelt at the altar with many other people. All I did was cry. I did not pray, and no one prayed with me. It was just something between me and God. He did something in me that night. That awful conviction lifted too! Oh, what a relief!

At the end of service, I was in the restroom and here came my friends saying, "I thought you were already saved!" I responded with, "I was," and didn't say anything else because I did not know what else to say. What I was afraid would happen with my peers did happen, but I no longer cared. I was so full of joy and peace because I had responded to the Lord.

I could not understand what had happened that night until I was much older and came to realize that God was asking me to publicly declare that I had decided to follow Jesus and had given my life to Him **in front of my peers**. This was a huge step in my life.

The next year I went to church camp. At this particular camp, they would announce all week that Thursday was Holy Spirit night, the night they invited campers to be filled with the Holy Spirit. They had everyone who wanted to be filled to come down front. The altar was full of kids wanting to receive. A camp leader came by and laid hands on my head and prayed over me. The words began to flow out of me freely and unhindered. I was filled with so much joy and peace. After the service was over, everyone went down to a campfire, but I sat on a swing for a long while, basking in the presence of God. I did not want to leave it.

Children really are able to sense God's presence which brings His love, joy, and peace. Once they get a taste of it, they just want more. I know because I experienced it as a child.

It should be our goal that when children come to the realization of sin and their need for a Savior that they will choose Jesus and step right on over into the Kingdom of God, making their time in the kingdom of darkness very brief. We must provide frequent opportunities for children to respond to accept Jesus as their Lord and Savior because we have no way of knowing when each child will come to this point in their lives.

Many times, we celebrate when the "worst of the worst" sinner gets saved, and we should do so because that is awesome. However, what a testimony it is to be able to say, **"I have lived for the Lord all my life and have never known anything else."** We should place as much value on such a testimony as that of the worst sinner who comes to the Lord. Every person who comes to Christ is to be celebrated! The angels in heaven celebrate! **Let's be intentional to celebrate and rejoice over every child who is saved too.**

Kalista's Story, as told by her mom

"When Kalista was around two years old, she came to me and said, 'Papa.' I told her that her papa and grandma were in the mountains. She said, 'No! Papa knee. Papa! Knee!' I asked, 'What about Papa's knee?' She said, 'Pay Papa knee.' 'Oh, we need to pray for Papa's knee?' I asked. 'Papa knee! Pay!' So we prayed for Papa's knee together.

When I spoke to Kalista's grandma later, she told me that Papa's knee had been hurting him, but then it suddenly quit hurting! I told her about when Kalista said to 'pay' for Papa's knee, and her grandma said that it was at that time that the pain had disappeared!" — *Lisa Mittas*

<u>Chelsea's Story, as told by her mom</u>

"In January of 1995, our family was vacationing in Florida. Towards the end of our stay, our seven-year-old daughter, Chelsea, fell off her bike, injuring her arm. She was in a lot of pain, so we took her to the emergency room at the local hospital. I remember that while praying over her, she was really howling in pain. The X-rays showed a hairline fracture in her forearm. The doctor put a splint around her arm, wrapped it, and put it in a sling. We were given the X-rays and told to schedule an appointment with the pediatrician when we returned to Ohio in a few days.

We had made plans to attend an All Faiths Crusade with Brother Hagin. The day before our flight home, we drove to Lakeland and went to the morning service where Bro. Hagin taught about prayer. I remember sitting in the balcony with Chelsea sitting on the floor at our feet playing during the long teaching. She was familiar with Brother Hagin because since she was a toddler, we often played a tape of him reciting healing scriptures in her bedroom at night.

After the service, we were returning to our hotel when Chelsea spotted an indoor playground called Discovery Zone. She told us that she wanted to go there. We told her that it wasn't a good idea because of her injury. She then told us that Bro. Hagin had just stated in the prayer teaching, 'If you are still praying for something that has already been covered in the Word, you are wasting your breath. You need to start claiming it as yours!' Wow! I didn't know that she was even paying attention! Honestly, I was doubtful but agreed to take off the splint and take her to Discovery Zone. I did not want to dismiss her childlike faith but wrestled with the thought of her further injuring her arm and being in a lot of pain. When we got to Discovery Zone, she just took off running and never looked back. She crawled, jumped, and hung from monkey bars, all without a single thought of her arm. The sling never went back on her arm. We took her to be re-examined in Ohio, and the X-ray showed no fracture. She was fine! I still keep the X-rays as a reminder of what childlike faith looks like." — *Mary Quigley*

Angie's Story

"In Christian circles, the question, "When did you get saved?" comes up often. My typical answer is, "I was born saved." I do not have any memory of praying the sinner's prayer because I was so young when I did (maybe 2-3 years old). I've always believed that Jesus died for my sins, rose from the grave, and lived in me.

When I was about four years old, I went outside to play on my swing set. It was one of those metal A-frame swing sets with two swings and a slide. I remember looking over at the other swing and seeing Jesus sitting next to me. All He did was smile at me. No words were spoken, but I remember His face clearly. His complete attention was on me. His smile said that He loved me with a love that was so much bigger than anything the world could offer me. It was a moment I have cherished my entire life.

My family attended a non-denominational church in northeast Ohio. I have fond memories of Bible stories told by felt board lessons and children's songs with lots of motions. As soon as I was old enough to help with the smallest task, I started serving in the church. I sang on stage and ran the overhead projector during services. I scrubbed toilets and sinks. I dusted and swept. I helped box groceries in the food pantry. I prepared and served meals for the elderly that came to our hot lunch program. I helped teach Children's Church and assisted the secretary with church office duties.

My life has had its challenges and rough moments, but through all of it, I have never doubted that I had a Father who loved me, a Savior who died for me, and a Helper living on the inside of me. I have never questioned or feared where I would go when I die. I have never panicked or worried about what was said on the news or which government leaders came into power. **I've never had to experience life without God**." — *Angela Fortney*

Discussion Questions

1. Is the Gospel being presented in a way that preschoolers and elementary-age children can understand and respond to the salvation message?

2. Are we providing frequent opportunities for children to accept Jesus as their Lord and Savior, and what does that look like?

Chapter 5
The Church of Today

"For his 'body' has been formed in his image and is closely joined together and constantly connected as one. And every member has been given divine gifts to contribute to the growth of all; and as these gifts operate effectively throughout the whole body, we are built up and made perfect in love." (Ephesians 4:16 TPT)

One of the popular sayings we have in the church world is that "Children are the Church of tomorrow." In one sense, that is true. They are the ones who will carry on the Gospel when we are gone, but **born-again children are just as much a part of the Church today as you and I**.

Children need to be taught and given opportunities to serve in the local church. Oftentimes, the best place for this is right in the children's classes. As vital as it is for a new believer to get hooked up with a local church and learn to serve, so it is with our children. Give them opportunities to be a part, grow, and develop the gifts God has placed inside of them.

Children have something to offer to the Body of Christ. The Holy Spirit is the One who connects us as believers. He is the One who puts gifts and callings in each of us. Every believer, including children, has something to bring to the Body. When children, preteens, and youth-age students have opportunities to serve in the local church, it will help them to stay connected and serve the Lord all of their lives.

But more importantly, they need to understand that by serving others they are really serving Father God. "...just like your faithful service is an offering to God" (Philippians 2:17b).

Here are some ideas where children can share their gifts:

- Worship team
- Prayer team
- Altar call team
- Tech team
- Audio team
- Greeters
- Clean-up team
- Helping with object lessons or props
- Puppets
- Outreach teams
- Leading a small group (with adult supervision)

There are many more ideas out there. Let the Holy Spirit give you divine ideas for teaching and training the children to find their gifts and their place in the local church.

Ephesians 4:16 (NKJV) "from whom the whole body, joined and knit together by what every joint supplies, according to the effective working by which every part does its share, causes growth of the body for the edifying of itself in love."

The way Christ designed the Church, His Body, is that every member has something to offer that the rest of the Body needs, and this includes born-again children who are our fellow brothers and sisters in the Lord.

However, before they can fully serve with the right heart, they must first become disciples. The moment we are born again we begin our relationship with Jesus. We need to take children beyond the born-again experience and teach them to become disciples of Jesus. Discipleship is more than saying "I believe in Jesus"; it is learning what His Word says and doing what it commands. This is where we as children's ministers come in. We are to teach them how to be disciples. Jesus said in John 14:15, "If you love me, obey my commandments."

When an adult is born again, what is their immediate need? They need to be discipled and taught the Word of God, including who they are in Christ and what He bought for them in His death, burial, and resurrection. Children need these things too, just the same as an adult. The difference is in how it is presented to them. You can put a steak in front of an adult and they can handle cutting and eating it, but with a child, you have to cut it into bite-sized pieces that are easy for them to chew and digest.

So it is with teaching children the Word. It is the same Word that we teach adults. It is just presented in smaller sizes and in different ways so that they can grasp and understand what is being taught. **When you feed a child the Word of God and help them get it in their hearts, you are**

giving the Holy Spirit something to work with in their lives.

In teaching the Word, personal testimonies of God's power can have a tremendous impact on the children. I remember a teacher in middle school sharing how the Lord had delivered her from an addiction to prescription nasal spray. At the time, being a dorky middle-schooler, I thought it was strange and forgot all about it. Around ten years later, the Holy Spirit brought that story back up to me. I had a bad sinus infection and was using nasal spray to open my sinus passages up. I would almost panic when they closed up and would quickly sniff that spray. One time as I was using the spray, the Holy Spirit reminded me of the story my teacher shared so long ago. I realized I was getting addicted to it. I put it down and said, "No, I'm not letting this control me." Isn't that amazing? The Holy Spirit was able to use a testimony from so long ago to help me. He will use the Word we are taught and the testimonies we hear from others to help us when we face trials and temptations.

Can you remember an instance where someone's personal story of God's power in their life impacted your life? Or can you remember a Bible lesson you learned as a child that the Holy Spirit used to help you later on?

If I can get one point across when it comes to teaching children, it is this: **GIVE THEM THE WORD OF GOD**. It is more than entertaining them, although you should use entertaining methods to bring across the message. Make it fun because kids love fun, and having fun makes it a positive experience for them and brings a sense of togetherness, keeping them engaged.

1 Corinthians 9:20-23 "When I was with the Jews, I lived like a Jew to bring the Jews to Christ. When I was with those who follow the Jewish law, I too lived under that law. Even though I am not subject to the law, I did this so I could bring to Christ those who are under the law. When I am with the Gentiles who do not follow the Jewish law, I too live apart from that law so I can bring them to Christ. But I do not ignore the law of God; I obey the law of Christ.

When I am with those who are weak, I share their weakness, for I want to bring the weak to Christ. Yes, I try to find common ground with everyone, doing everything I can to save some. I do everything to spread the Good News and share in its blessings."

What Paul is saying here is he changed up his methods to reach and teach people based on their life experiences while never compromising the Word or his principles. He adapted to what they needed so they were able to understand his message. We should employ the same principles in teaching children.

The following statistics are from the book *The Bridger Generation* by Thom S. Rainer:

- Builders (born 1927-1945): 65% Bible-based believers
- Boomers (born 1946-1964): 35% Bible-based believers
- Busters (born 1965-1983): 16% Bible-based believers
- Bridgers (or Millennials, born 1984 or later): 4% Bible-based believers[1]

Many people call themselves Christians, but today only 4% of Christian Millennials are Bible-believers. These statistics are a critical reason why children need to be taught the truth from the Bible. Each child has their own relationship with Christ, independent of their parents, so they need to be able to defend their faith when it is challenged by an ungodly worldview. Now, more than ever, children need to be led by the Holy Spirit in every aspect of their lives to navigate these highly unusual times.

Acts 2:17, 39 "'In the last days,' God says, 'I will pour out my Spirit upon all people. Your sons and daughters will prophesy. Your young men will see visions, and your old men will dream dreams.'"

"This promise is to you, to your children, and to those far away—all who have been called by the Lord our God."

Children are not excluded in these promises. The promise of the Holy Spirit is for all believers!

John 16:13-15 "When the Spirit of truth comes, he will guide you into all truth. He will not speak on his own but will tell you what he has heard. He will bring me glory by telling you whatever he receives from me. All that belongs to the Father is mine; this is why I said, 'The Spirit will tell you whatever he receives from me.'"

The Holy Spirit came to help, counsel, teach, and empower the children to be the Church of Today.

Finally, remember that the children in your classes will have different callings and assignments in the future. Some may be called to pastor. Some may be called to missions or to be an evangelist. You may have the next Billy Graham, Kathryn Kuhlman, Aimee Semple McPherson, Christine Caine, Charles Spurgeon, John Wesley, or George Whitefield sitting right there among the children. It is a great honor to be trusted by our Father God to impart the Word into their lives that will prepare them for their call.

Shawna's Story

"Like most people, I have limited memories of my childhood. But looking back, there are several moments that have never left my memory. I was six years old, and we had just come home from church. My little sister and I were playing in our family's unfinished basement when we were called upstairs. My sister ran up the steps, but I lagged behind. I remember I was wearing my favorite purple shirt and swinging in circles around one of the poles in the basement as I smiled, thinking about church earlier that morning. Today felt special. Today I got saved. I knew that meant that I'd be going to heaven, and that meant Jesus was always with me. As I swung in circles, I looked up and thought, 'I wonder if God really heard me when I prayed in church this morning to ask Him into my heart.' I started feeling nervous that maybe He hadn't heard me since several other kids raised their hands in class that morning. So right there in my basement (where I had His undivided attention), I prayed again, asking Jesus to come into my heart. I remember feeling like He was actually in that basement with me. I genuinely felt His presence, and I smiled, thinking, 'Well, now He'll always be with me!'

When I was seven years old, my mom was tucking me into bed, and, as most children do, I began asking her questions to put off going to sleep. She answered them patiently and even encouraged more conversation. I remember her taking extra time talking to me that night, and we began talking about the Holy Spirit. In church, they were talking about Him, and I told my mom I felt left out because I hadn't raised my hand to be filled but wanted to. She prayed with me right there, and I began speaking in other tongues for the first time. Almost 25 years later, as I tucked my five-year-old daughter into bed and she began asking me questions about Jesus and salvation, I felt a nudge from the Holy Spirit to take the extra time with her that night, much like my mom had done with me. My daughter and I prayed

together as she asked Jesus into her heart." — *Shawna
Whittaker*

Discussion Questions

1. Are those who were part of our Children's Ministry
   continuing to attend church through high school,
   college, and as adults?

2. How can we give our children an opportunity to
   identify and use their gifts to serve the church from a
   young age?

3. Are we teaching them how to use their Bible and
   apply it to their lives?

Chapter 6
Help! I Need Help!

"Be anxious for nothing, but in everything by prayer and supplication, with thanksgiving, let your requests be made known to God."
(Philippians 4:6 NKJV)

"How can I get people to help us, and how can I get them to stay?" This question is one I receive often. I do not claim to be an expert in this area, but I can tell you what I did.

The first thing is to pray, pray, pray! I did a lot of praying for the Lord to send people to help us reach the children. My prayer was, "Lord, send us people with clean hands and a pure heart; hands that would never harm a child and a heart with the right motives. Lord, stir the hearts of people to help and, if necessary, bring them to our church if they aren't already here." God sure answered this prayer and sent many marvelous people who had the Father's heart for children and were gifted with talents and the anointing to minister to them.

You must qualify those who serve and have a screening process which includes an application, references, an interview, and a background check. There can be legal ramifications if you don't screen them.

It makes me cringe when churches take anyone to help in the children's classes just because they are upright and breathing. Recruit people in person and teach your volunteers to do the same. Rarely is a plea from the pulpit or in the announcements effective. Instead, share the good things that are happening and positive testimonies of God working in the lives of children. People want to be a part of something that is positive and making a difference.

Make sure to communicate the honor it is to be a part of this ministry. Begging people to help in the children's classes is not appealing to anyone. Recruit like Jesus; He called them one by one.

Do not overlook the vast resources of preteens and teens to help, under two-adult-deep supervision of course. This is a great place for them to use their gifts. They have an excitement and energy that older generations do not have. We need them. The children need them, and the teens need to be valued. You will see how quickly the children will look up to and emulate the teens who are serving in their class.

Be prepared when the people come to serve. Don't waste their time. You need to be able to communicate the vision and value of children's ministry. Be ready to train them on the guidelines you have established for running the classes and maintaining safety and security.

Make sure you do not overwhelm people by giving them a lot of responsibility right away. I made this mistake in the early years and regretted it. Gradually release responsibility to people and prove them first. Conversely, some children's ministry leaders have a tendency to try to do everything themselves. I encourage you to empower others who are serving with you. Jesus could not do it all by Himself and neither can you. He duplicated Himself in His disciples and then sent them out.

As I stated in the Preface, you have to keep the vision before those who serve with you. Habakkuk 2:2 (NKJV) tells us to "Write the vision and make it plain..." Keep reminding your people that this is precious to our Father's heart.

Here is a side note: **your vision for children's ministry must line up with your pastor's vision for the church**. Every church has its own unique calling and assignment, and that will translate to all the ministry areas in the church. You are not just doing your own thing. You are a part of the bigger picture of your local church. Here is an example of what I am referring to: Our church's vision is "Go, Grow, Give." Every program we have is designed to accomplish this. We took these directives and applied them to our Generational Ministries from the nursery up through college age. The wins defined for each department have to fit in our church's vision.

A pastor is called to reach all ages of people in his/her community. Your Children's Ministry serves as an extension of the pastor to fulfill this call in reaching the children.

A key for volunteer retention is allowing them to have an open door for ideas, questions, and issues they may have. Some of the best ideas we ever received came from our volunteer team. For example, one of our volunteers, Cookie Jevec, came up with an idea for recruiting more help for the nurseries while allowing our older population to serve without being overly taxed physically. She called it "Rocking Angels." They are given the opportunity to volunteer during a service if we just need a baby rocked, held, or fed. We simply put up a call number so they know we need their help. They pray over the babies and speak words of life to them. They do not have to change diapers or get down on the floor, but this provides additional nursery support when needed. It also provides an opportunity for our older generation to use their gifts. It has been very successful.

This idea came from a volunteer, not leadership, so keep an open mind, open door, and an open ear to these Holy-Spirit-inspired ideas. Children's ministry is not a dictatorship. It is a team effort. We should never be of the mindset that "It's my way or the highway." You may lose people faster than you can blink.

Communication is vital to a healthy volunteer team. You need to communicate any changes and important information well in advance. I have seen volunteers very frustrated when clear communication was not received in a timely manner from their leaders. You will lose people if you do not communicate well. If it does not come naturally to you, then work on it and become good at it. Ask someone who is a good communicator to help you.

Another key to volunteer retention is to recognize and reward your volunteers. Let them know you see them serving and how much you appreciate them. Talk to them about the rewards Jesus has in store for them as well. (More on this in the next chapter). Celebrate the praise reports and testimonies with all the volunteers so that they understand they are a part of something amazing.

A wonderful idea is to have a prayer group dedicated to praying for the generational ministry in your church. They can pray as often as once a week or once a month. You can communicate urgent prayer requests to them any time, even when you aren't meeting. Prayer changes things, so don't neglect the power of getting other people to pray with you for the ministry and the team. People praying do not even need to be a part of the children's ministry. There are people whose way to serve the children is by praying for them.

Make sure that you are keeping yourself fed and built up spiritually by attending the adult service to sit under the anointing of your pastor. You can listen to or watch a message later if you are serving. However, you absolutely need to get in there on a routine basis because there is something about corporate worship in the company of other believers and the anointing that is on your pastor that cannot be replaced by listening to a sermon or watching online. **Your pastor is equipping you for the work of the ministry.**

Keep up your own daily fellowship with the Lord and the Word. Anytime I have been frazzled, worn out, or frustrated, it was usually because I had neglected these things. In the early years, when I was still learning to lead, I would miss getting into service as much as six weeks at a time. This is so unhealthy, and it was the worst thing I could do. I wish someone would have come to me and smacked me silly for doing that. I have heard several different children's ministers tell me that they felt out of place in the adult sanctuary because they were rarely in there. That is a huge *"red flag"* warning you that there is a big problem and you better fix it fast, or you will burn out and get out of the will of God.

If you are the leader, do not let anyone on your team get into this condition. It is the Father's heart that we care for and nurture our team members.

To learn more about training, growing, and caring for your volunteers, read *The Red Book: The Life Blood of Children's Ministry* by Mark Harper. It will be immensely helpful for your ministry.

Declan's Story, as told by his mom

"Recently, Courtney Jacobs posted a video of her daughter Londyn, age 10, singing the song 'Promises.' Londyn has a beautiful voice like her mom. My boys repeatedly asked to watch this video. My son, Declan, who is 4, wanted to learn this song, so he could sing it too. How amazing is it that I get to watch God's faithfulness to me (they are miracle children) sing about God's faithfulness!" — *Sarah Chester*

(This story demonstrates the tremendous influence that preteens and teenagers can have on the younger generation and why we need them to be a part of our children's ministry.)

Kalista's Story Part 2

"When I was four years old, I gave my life to Jesus. Although I was very young when I accepted Christ, in my spirit I knew exactly what I was doing. My leaders in Children's Church from a young age helped me become familiar with the presence of God, so when it came time, and I was old enough to understand, my spirit had already been prepped for four years. I think the biggest blessing of my life has been to never know a day without Him close. When I think of my early years, I am reminded of moments in His presence learning of who He is. Ever since I received Jesus, I have always had a deep desire to follow Him and know Him more every day of my life. Part of that was getting involved serving at my church. As soon as I was 11 years old, I began serving in children's church and served there until I was 19 years old.

During that period, when I was 13, I went to a youth conference our church held. We had a moment in worship where we got to rest in His presence and let Him speak to us. I remember standing on the left side of the room holding my hands out in front of me, palms up, listening for His voice. In that moment, I asked the Lord about my calling. I first said under my breath, 'school teacher,' and listened. I didn't hear anything. I'm not even sure why I said what I said next but then under my breath I said, 'ministry,' and the Lord spoke almost audibly to my spirit. Although it was not audible, it was so loud inside of me that I was called to the ministry that it felt like I heard it with my natural ears. That day I knew without a doubt in my mind that I was called to ministry. What that would look like, I wasn't sure yet. There has not been a day since then that I have questioned being called to ministry. Since that moment, every time I ask the Lord about what ministry will look like, He always has responded, 'Stay close to Me.' In addition, I have always known the significance of serving in the local church. I can guarantee that I would not be where I am without serving.

No matter the season, my life has always been about staying close to Him. It has been a daily discipline and determination in my heart. Once I graduated high school, I knew I was supposed to continue serving at my church, which led me to participate in an accredited college program through the church. I got hands-on ministry experience in high school and college ministry, and now I have a job at my church working in our high school and college department. Although it is not the final destination by any means, I know that no matter what it looks like, I am to stay close to Him."
— *Kalista Mittas*

Discussion Questions

1. Do we have a solid system in place...

- To directly recruit new adult and youth volunteers?
- To qualify everyone who wants to serve?
- For ongoing training?
- To cast vision?

2. Are we sharing and celebrating the good things happening in our classes and stories of God working in the lives of the children? Who should we be sharing these with?

Chapter 7
Don't Give Up

"So let's not get tired of doing what is good. At just the right time we will reap a harvest of blessing if we don't give up." (Galatians 6:9)

One thing I know from personal experience is that this branch of ministry is hard work—physically, mentally, and emotionally. We are caring for a great variety of personalities and needs of the children, as well as communicating with their families.

Once I was driving down a road near my house. As I passed by a large strawberry farm, I heard these words on the inside: "Children are like strawberries." I immediately understood what the Holy Spirit was saying to me. I remembered when we were kids, mom took my siblings and me to that very field to pick strawberries. She would assign each of us to a row, and we picked lots of berries (and maybe would sneak a few to eat). When you pick strawberries, you get down on your hands and knees and pick the berries one by one, being careful not to crush or bruise the fruit. When dealing with children, we must also be careful not to crush or bruise their little minds and spirits. That's how it is in this branch of ministry. It is much more labor-intensive than other ministries. You might have to get on the floor with the little ones or hold and rock the babies. You might have to jump around when singing a song with the older kids. It is a great degree of physical work, but the Holy Spirit is saying that the reward is sweet and precious.

I remember in the early years of our church, when we were growing so fast, we hardly had room for all we needed to do. On Wednesday nights, the Youth Group used the Kindergarten room, so I would have ages 5 to 12 crammed in one small room. I was not good at recruiting back then and oftentimes just didn't have enough help.

Children are not always perfect little angels. They like to test boundaries. There were a few nights I left the building and sat in my car and cried because it had been such a rough night. Actually, this happened a lot more than I would like to admit.

Once, after a particularly grueling night, I decided to quit. I was going to march into the sanctuary, find the pastor and let him know I was done; he could find someone else. I was still a volunteer at that point and working a full-time job. The children's ministry had grown so much that, in essence, I was working two jobs at the same time.

I entered the sanctuary and stomped my way up front to talk to the pastor. When I got up there, it was as if the Holy Ghost slapped His hand across my mouth, and I couldn't speak. I whirled around and quickly walked out. Thank goodness our pastor was talking with someone else and did not notice his crazy Children's Pastor at that moment in time. I am so grateful the Holy Spirit stopped me. I would have missed out on the precious fruit of children being saved, filled with the Holy Spirit, and trained to be disciples. I would have missed out on pleasing our Father because this is so important to Him.

Sometimes encouragement came from other people, especially my husband, Jay. He was always supportive. He never complained when I was gone every night during the week leading up to a big project or all the nights I was away practicing with our puppet team.

The best encourager of all was always the Holy Spirit. When I was overwhelmed or having a bad attitude and wanted to quit, He would always speak up in my heart and say, "Who are you doing this for?" I would reply, "I'm doing this for Jesus." My attitude would be corrected when I remembered why I was doing all the hard work. That one little heart adjustment gave me the strength and the joy to carry on.

You will not always hear "thank you" from kids or parents or even your leaders. If you are only going to serve because you are looking for a pat on the back, you will be disappointed. You cannot do anything in the Kingdom of God, including children's ministry, for the praise and recognition of man. It is really nice when you get it, but that cannot be your motivation. You should be able to keep going even if you never hear a "thank you" from another person because ultimately, you are doing this for Jesus. This is important to Him and precious to Father God.

Leaders, remember that not everyone will be in the place spiritually where they can serve without being recognized and thanked, so be intentional to notice what they are doing and thank them. Point out the good they are doing and let them contribute with their ideas and have input in what you are doing in your children's ministry. They will feel valued when you do.

It's okay to talk to your team about the reward because the Bible talks about reward. Sometimes we just need that encouragement. For me personally, **the greatest reward I can receive is to hear Jesus say, "Well done, good and faithful servant." I only want to please Him.**

Jesus said these words:

> **Matthew 10:40, 42** "Anyone who receives you receives me, and anyone who receives me receives the Father who sent me… And if you give even a cup of cold water to one of the least of my followers, you will surely be rewarded."
>
> **Matthew 25:40** "And the King will say, 'I tell you the truth, when you did it to one of the least of these my brothers and sisters, you were doing it to me!'"
>
> **Mark 9:36-37** "Then he put a little child among them. Taking the child in his arms, he said to them, 'Anyone who welcomes a little child like this on my behalf welcomes me, and anyone who welcomes me welcomes not only me but also my Father who sent me.'"

Wow! This is amazing! Jesus said that if we welcome a little child on His behalf, it is the same thing as if we welcomed Jesus into our classroom, and if we welcome Jesus, then it is the same as if we welcomed Father God. Remember this when you are ministering to the children.

Are you rocking a baby in the nursery? Are you comforting a crying child? Are you giving a child a drink of water? Are you speaking words of life and encouragement to a child? Are you changing a stinky diaper? Are you telling them the good news about what Jesus did for them? **You are not just doing it to that individual child; you are doing it to Jesus.** That is exactly how He sees it. Yes, there is even a reward for changing the stinky diaper when you do it with the right attitude and a loving heart as a representative of Jesus.

You will never miss out on what God is doing in the church when you are serving the babies and children. It used to infuriate me when people would come to get their children after the adult service and tell our volunteers that they had missed out because the service in the adult sanctuary had been so good. That could have been discouraging for our volunteers to hear. I guarantee that you will not miss out on anything because you are serving God's kids! Father God is good, and He will make sure you receive everything you need.

Much of what we do in Children's Ministry is behind the scenes. Most of it will never be seen by people outside the classroom, but Jesus sees it. Jesus is keeping a record of all the things you are doing for Him in His name. He sees all the time you spend in prayer and preparation for your class. The children are precious to Him and Father God. He is not going to let your love and sacrifice to reach, teach, and disciple them go unnoticed. It all matters, and you matter to Jesus. He is pleased with you.

Children really are precious in His sight, so do not give up! Keep going! There is a marvelous reward and great joy in store for you, and never forget that heaven is watching.

> **Hebrews 12:1** "Therefore, since we are surrounded by such a huge crowd of witnesses to the life of faith, let us strip off every weight that slows us down, especially the sin that so easily trips us up. And let us run with endurance the race God has set before us."

I also want to stress this point: **you are not to minister to the babies and children in your own ability and strength alone**. Depend on the anointing of the Holy Spirit in you and on you. Jesus declared over Himself, *"The Spirit of the Lord is upon me, for he has anointed me to bring Good news to the poor. He has sent me to proclaim that captives will be released, that the blind will see, that the oppressed will be set free, and that the time of the Lord's favor has come"* (Luke 4:18-19).

Because we belong to Jesus, the same anointing that is on Him as the Head of the Body of Christ is on us, as members of the Body of Christ. If Jesus declared that He was anointed, we can declare that we are anointed. Speak this scripture over yourself before you get into a classroom. This way, you are depending on the Holy Spirit to help you and work through you to change the lives of the children you will come into contact with. I like to declare over myself, "**The Spirit**

of the Lord is on me to minister His life, His love, and His Word to the children." This puts your dependence on Him and not yourself. It also helps you to keep the right perspective when you are tempted to grow weary and quit.

One last note for pastors, deacons, and church leaders: If you minister to the little ones who cannot repay you, then Father God, who is the great rewarder, will repay you. Children are not going to be able to support the church financially, but God will take care of you. Your goal should be for all the children to be saved, grow up in the Word, and become committed members of your church. If we only serve the ones who can repay us, there is no reward in it. The truth is that these children will grow up, and if we have done our job correctly, they will be actively serving and tithing members of our church. As Reverend Ken Blount says, "If you want an exciting church that is full of life... invest in the youth and children's ministries! They can't pay you back, but Jesus will."[1]

Someday, we will stand before Jesus to receive our reward. I believe that many people will be surprised by the ones who get the greatest reward. Many are going to be the people who spent all those hours pouring out Jesus' love on the babies and the children because this is so precious to Father God and to our Lord Jesus. "But anyone who obeys God's law **and teaches them will be called great in the Kingdom of Heaven**" (Matthew 5:19b). Soul winners will have a special reward, too. If you are winning children to

Jesus, you are a soul winner. Well done, good and faithful servant.[1]

Discussion Questions

1. Are we making sure that we, as a team, are staying built up and connected to the vision of our pastor?

2. How can we better encourage our volunteers to not grow weary in running the race set before them?

3. Is prayer an integral part of our support system?

Endnotes

Preface - Why This Book?

[1]Roy Rogers and Dale Evans, "Jesus Loves the Little Children," on *Jesus Loves the Little Children*, Golden Records, 1956, compact disc.

Chapter 1 - The Challenge We Face

[1]Tom Toney, speech on clarity and organizational alignment (Clarity, Alignment, and Busting Barriers, shared at Faith Family Church, North Canton, OH, February 14, 2019).

[2]"When Americans Become Christians", National Association of Evangelicals, Spring 2015. https://www.nae.net/when-americans-become-christians/ (accessed July 5, 2019).

[3]George Barna, *Transforming Children into Spiritual Champions: Why Children Should Be Your Church's #1 Priority* (Grand Rapids, MI: Baker Books, 2016), p. 18, 35.

[4]Ken Blount Ministries, "If you want an exciting church that is full of life... invest in the youth and children's ministries! They can't pay you back, but Jesus will," Facebook, February 26, 2019, 3:10 p.m., https://www.facebook.com/kenblountministries/posts/2158603750863968.

[5]The World Bank, https://data.worldbank.org/indicator/SP.POP.0014.TO.ZS

Chapter 2 - Our Heavenly Father's Perspective

[1]https://www.christianquotes.info/images/charles-spurge3-ways-better-christian-parent/

Chapter 3 - Our Responsibility

[1]Ronald Reagan, "Encroaching Control," March 30, 1961, Internet Archive, MP3 audio (43:29), https://archive.org/details/RonaldReagan-EncroachingControl.

[2]Ken Blount Ministries, "As a parent, the greatest teacher your children have is the life for Christ you are living in front of them, through the good and bad times in life," Facebook, January 15, 2019, 7:57 AM, https://www.facebook.com/kenblountministries/posts/2096443963746614?__tn__=-R.

[3]RhemaUSA. "10.25.20 | Sun. 10am | Rev. Kenneth W. Hagin." YouTube video, 1:45:30, October 25, 2020. https://www.youtube.com/watch?v=lgWPeubfnSM.

Chapter 4 - Are They Too Young?

[1]https://www.quotetab.com/quote/by-charles-spurgeon/a-child-of-five-if-properly-instructed-can-as-truly-believe-and-be-regenerate?source=children

Chapter 5 - The Church of Today

[1]Jerry Moyer, "Why is The Jubilee Gang a multi-media ministry?" Facebook, February 22, 2019, 8:47 AM, https://www.facebook.com/Jubileegang/posts/10216807239946859.

[2]Thom S. Rainer, *The Bridger Generation: America's Second Largest Generation, What They Believe, How to Reach Them* (Nashville, TN: Broadman and Holman Publishers, 1997).

Chapter 7 - Don't Give Up

[1]Matthew 25:23 (NKJV)

Made in the USA
Columbia, SC
06 March 2021